T

A LION BOOK
Oxford · Batavia · Sydney

Long ago in Israel people were waiting for a special baby – God's promised King – to be born. And there were others, in distant lands a long way to the east, who also hoped for the birth of this new king.

Wise men called astronomers studied the stars and planets looking for signs in the sky that might show something unusual was going to happen.

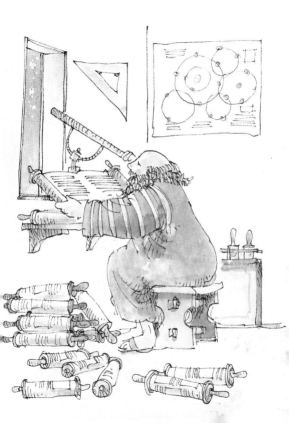

One night a very bright star shone in the sky.

"Look," said one of the wise men. "There is a new star. I have never seen that one before. It is shining more brightly than any of the others. I wonder what it can mean?"

The astronomers looked in their scrolls to find out if the bright star was a sign of something special.

"Such a star may mean that a great king has been born," said one of the wise men. "Perhaps it is the promised King we have been waiting for."

"We must follow the star and find out," said another.

The wise men packed up food and clothing for a long journey.

Then they loaded up their camels and set off towards the land over which the star seemed to shine.

They carried with them rich presents ready to give to the new king.

For a long time they travelled, until
at last, tired and weary, they came to
the land of Israel.

"We must go to Jerusalem," said
one of the wise men. "The king's
palace will be in that city."

And so they made their way to the
palace to search for the new-born king.

When they reached the palace they met King Herod. He was a greedy and jealous man who ruled over the land of Israel by order of the mighty Roman Emperor.

The wise men told King Herod why they had come. When he heard about a new king, Herod was secretly very angry and upset. He did not want anyone to take away his power.

But Herod did not show the wise men he was worried. He pretended to be pleased. He wanted the astronomers to find the new king so that he could kill him.

Herod knew of an ancient promise that a special king would be born in the town of Bethlehem.

"Go on with your search," he said to the wise men. "Go to Bethlehem. And when you find the new king, come and tell me where he is so that I can take him presents too."

So the wise men set off towards the little town of Bethlehem. All the time they were following the star.

"The ancient prophets of Israel said this is where the new King and Saviour would be born," said one of the wise men.

"And look, the star is shining brightly overhead," said another.

The wise men's journey had taken many weeks.

By the time they arrived in Bethlehem Mary and Joseph had moved from the cave where Jesus was born. They were living in a little house until Mary and the baby were ready to travel back to Nazareth.

That night the astronomers walked through the streets of the little town searching for the place where the baby could be.

At last they came to Mary and Joseph's home.

"Look, the star is right overhead," said one of the wise men.

"This must surely be the house," said another.

So they knocked gently on the door.

Then the wise men entered the tiny house. It was poor and simple – not at all like the rich palace they had expected.

They went in and there they saw Joseph and Mary, who was holding the baby Jesus in her arms.

When they saw the child the wise men knelt down and worshipped him.

"At last we have found the Promised
One, the new-born King," they said.

And they gave the baby Jesus their rich
gifts of gold, frankincense and myrrh.

Afterwards the wise men left the
little family in peace and rested for a
while before their long journey
home to the East.

That night as they slept God warned the wise men not to return to Herod.

So the next day the astronomers chose a different route home. And they set off once more to the far-off land where they lived, rejoicing that they had seen the King.

Text copyright © 1990 Carol Watson
Illustrations copyright © 1990 Toni Goffe

Published by
**Lion Publishing plc**
Sandy Lane West, Oxford,
England
ISBN 0 7459 1867 0
**Lion Publishing Corporation**
1705 Hubbard Avenue, Batavia,
Illinois 60510, USA
ISBN 0 7459 1867 0
**Albatross Books Pty Ltd**
PO Box 320, Sutherland, NSW 2232,
Australia
ISBN 0 7324 0175 5

First edition 1990
Reprinted 1991

Printed and bound in Singapore